Biodiversity
of Oceans and Seas

GREG PYERS

MACMILLAN
LIBRARY

First published in 2011 by
MACMILLAN EDUCATION AUSTRALIA PTY LTD
15–19 Claremont Street, South Yarra 3141

Visit our website at www.macmillan.com.au or go directly to www.macmillanlibrary.com.au

Associated companies and representatives throughout the world.

National Library of Australia Cataloguing-in-Publication entry

Pyers, Greg.
   Of oceans / Greg Pyers.
   ISBN: 9781420278835 (hbk.)
   Biodiversity.
   Includes index.
   For primary school age.
   Ocean—Juvenile literature. Biodiversity conservation—Juvenile literature.

577.7

Publisher: Carmel Heron
Commissioning Editor: Niki Horin
Managing Editor: Vanessa Lanaway
Editor: Georgina Garner
Proofreader: Tim Clarke
Designer: Kerri Wilson
Page layout: Raul Diche
Photo researcher: Wendy Duncan (management: Debbie Gallagher)
Illustrator: Richard Morden
Production Controller: Vanessa Johnson

Printed in China

Acknowledgements
The author and publisher are grateful to the following for permission to reproduce copyright material:

Front cover photograph: sharks swimming over reef, Fiji, courtesy of Getty Images/Flickr/Alexander Safonov.
Back cover photographs courtesy of Shutterstock/Computer Earth (whale), /Drabovich Olga (shell).

Photographs courtesy of:
ANTphoto.com.au/Barbara Todd, **7**; Australian Customs and Border Protection Service, © Commonwealth of Australia,
reproduced by permission, **25**; Corbis/Daniel J. Cox, **15**, /Sandro Vannini, **29**; Getty Images/Flickr/Alexander Safonov, **14**,
National Geographic/David Doubilet, **8**, /Time & Life Pictures/Stan Wayman, **20**, /Stone/Arnulf Husmo, **24**; istockphoto/Ian
Scott, **13**; photolibrary/Alamy/Maximilian Weinzierl, **28**, /Alamy/Poelzer Wolfgang, **27**, /OSF/Tony & Sheila Phelps, **17**, /Science
Photo Library/Georgette Douwma, **22**; Picture Media/Reuters/Queensland Museum/Gary Cranitch, **10**; Shutterstock/Rich Carey,
4. Background and design images used throughout courtesy of Shutterstock/Sergey Popov V (dive), /EpicStock (wave).

Other material: Diagrams showing effect of climate change courtesy of CSIRO Australia, **23**.

While every care has been taken to trace and acknowledge copyright, the publisher tenders their apologies for any accidental
infringement where copyright has proved untraceable. They would be pleased to come to a suitable arrangement with the rightful
owner in each case.

Please note
At the time of printing, the Internet addresses appearing in this book were correct. Owing to the dynamic nature of the Internet,
however, we cannot guarantee that all these addresses will remain correct.

Contents

Glossary words

When a word is printed in **bold**, you can look up its meaning in the Glossary on page 31.

What is biodiversity?

Biodiversity, or biological diversity, describes the variety of living things in a particular place, in a particular **ecosystem** or across the whole Earth.

Measuring biodiversity

The biodiversity of a particular area is measured on three levels:

- **species** diversity, which is the number and variety of species in the area
- genetic diversity, which is the variety of **genes** each species has. Genes determine the characteristics of different living things. A variety of genes within a species enables it to **adapt** to changes in its environment.
- ecosystem diversity, which is the variety of **habitats** in the area. A diverse ecosystem has many habitats within it.

Species diversity

Some habitats, such as coral reefs and rainforests, have very high biodiversity. One scientific study found 534 species in 5 square metres of coral reef in the Caribbean Sea. In the Amazon rainforest, in South America, 50 species of ants and many other species were found in just 1 square metre of leaf litter. In desert habitats, the same area might be home to as few as 10 species.

Habitats and ecosystems

Oceans and seas are habitats, which are places where plants and animals live. Within an ocean or sea habitat, there are also many smaller habitats, sometimes called microhabitats. Some ocean and sea habitats are sandy sea floors, rocky reefs and **seamounts**. Different kinds of **organisms** live in these places. The animals, plants, other living things and non-living things and all the ways they affect each other make up an ocean or sea ecosystem.

Turtles, fish and corals are part of ocean biodiversity.

4

Biodiversity under threat

The variety of species on Earth is under threat. There are somewhere between 5 million and 30 million species on Earth. Most of these species are very small and hard to find, so only about 1.75 million species have been described and named. These are called known species.

Scientists estimate that as many as 50 species become **extinct** every day. Extinction is a natural process, but human activities have sped up the rate of extinction by up to 1000 times.

Known species of organisms on Earth

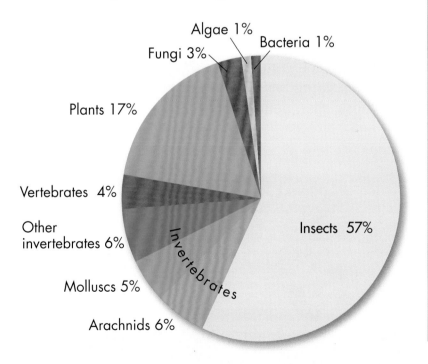

Algae 1%
Bacteria 1%
Fungi 3%
Plants 17%
Vertebrates 4%
Other invertebrates 6%
Insects 57%
Molluscs 5%
Invertebrates
Arachnids 6%

The known species of organisms on Earth can be divided into bacteria, algae, fungi, plant and animal species. Animal species are classified as vertebrates or invertebrates.

Approximate numbers of known vertebrate species

ANIMAL GROUP	KNOWN SPECIES
Fish	31 000
Birds	10 000
Reptiles	8 800
Amphibians	6 500
Mammals	5 500

Why is biodiversity important?

Biodiversity is important for many reasons. The diverse **organisms** in an **ecosystem** take part in natural processes essential to the survival of all living things. Biodiversity produces food and medicine. It is also important to people's quality of life.

Natural processes

Humans are part of many ecosystems. Our survival depends on the natural processes that go on in these ecosystems. Through natural processes, air and water are cleaned, waste is decomposed, **nutrients** are recycled and disease is kept under control. Natural processes depend on the organisms that live in the soil, on the plants that produce oxygen and absorb **carbon dioxide**, and on the organisms that break down dead plants and animals. When **species** of organisms become **extinct**, natural processes may stop working.

Food

We depend on biodiversity for our food. The world's major food plants are grains, vegetables and fruits. These plants have all been bred from plants in the wild. Wild plants are important sources of **genes** for breeding new disease-resistant crops. If these wild plants were to become extinct, their genes would be lost.

Medicine

About 40 per cent of all prescription drugs come from chemicals that have been extracted from plants. Scientists discover new, useful plant chemicals every year. The United States National Cancer Institute discovered that 70 per cent of plants found to have anti-cancer properties were rainforest plants. When plant species become extinct, the chemicals within them are lost forever. The lost chemicals may have been important in the making of new medicines.

Did you know?

About one-fifth of all animal **protein** eaten by humans comes from the sea. In Asia, one billion people rely on **marine** animals as their main source of protein.

Quality of life

Biodiversity is important to people's quality of life. Animals and plants inspire wonder. They are part of our **heritage**. The largest animal ever, the blue whale, still survives in the world's oceans and seas, despite being hunted almost to extinction. Very few people have ever seen a blue whale, but the knowledge that it still exists is uplifting.

Extinct species

Steller's sea cow was a relative of dugongs and manatees, and it lived in the coastal seas of the northern Pacific Ocean. It weighed up to 10 000 kilograms. In 1741, Europeans first saw the sea cow and they began to hunt it for its oil, flesh and skin. By 1768, Steller's sea cow was extinct.

Whales are one example of how biodiversity inspires people's wonder and imagination and improves our quality of life.

Oceans and seas of the world

Oceans are vast expanses of water that cover around 70 per cent of Earth's surface. Within an ocean, there are areas called seas. Oceans and seas may be warm or cold, deep or shallow. These characteristics affect their biodiversity.

Oceans

The world has five oceans, which are the Pacific, Atlantic, Indian, Southern and Arctic oceans. The Pacific and Atlantic oceans have cold waters in the north and south, near the Arctic and the Antarctic, and they have warm waters in **tropical** areas. The Southern and Arctic oceans are cold-water oceans, and the Indian Ocean is a warm-water ocean.

Ocean areas

OCEAN	AREA (SQUARE KILOMETRES)	DEEPEST POINT (METRES BELOW SEA LEVEL)	LENGTH OF COASTLINE (KILOMETRES)
Pacific Ocean	155 557 000	Marianas Trench (10 924)	135 663
Atlantic Ocean	76 762 000	Puerto Rico Trench (8 605)	111 866
Indian Ocean	68 556 000	Sunda Trench (7 258)	66 526
Southern Ocean	20 327 000	South Sandwich Trench (7 235)	17 968
Arctic Ocean	14 056 000	Fram Basin (4 665)	45 329

The Sargasso Sea is part of the Atlantic Ocean. It is known for the large amounts of sargassum seaweed that float on its surface. Many of the animal species that live there eat and shelter among the seaweed.

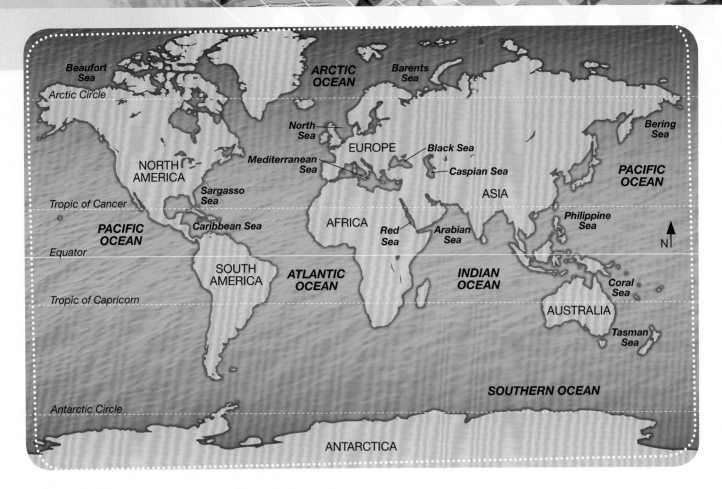

This map shows the world's five oceans and just some of its seas.

Seas

A sea may be part of an ocean or separate from an ocean. The Coral Sea and the Tasman Sea are part of the Pacific Ocean, and the Caribbean Sea and the North Sea are part of the Atlantic Ocean. The Mediterranean Sea, the Red Sea and the Caspian Sea are not part of any ocean.

Like an ocean, a sea may be tropical or **temperate**, shallow or deep. These physical characteristics affect the types of animals and plants that live in the sea. The Coral Sea is shallow and warm, so many corals grow there. The corals build coral reefs, which are **habitats** for many **species** of fish. In deep, cold seas, such as the Tasman Sea, fish species such as the slow-growing orange roughy can be found.

The Caspian Sea

The Caspian Sea, in Asia, is the largest **landlocked** body of water in the world. It was formed 5.5 million years ago, when movement of Earth's crust and a fall in sea levels cut it off from other seas. Today, its water is only one-third as salty as sea water elsewhere, and only species that can survive in slightly salty water live there. This is one reason why the biodiversity of the Caspian Sea is less than half that of the nearby Black Sea, which is not landlocked.

Ocean and sea biodiversity

There are about 230 000 known **marine species**, but not all of the oceans have been explored and scientists think there may be as many as one million marine species. Underwater structures such as **seamounts** are areas of rich biodiversity.

Studying ocean and sea biodiversity

Only 5 per cent of the oceans have been explored thoroughly, and scientists are still making discoveries about ocean and sea biodiversity. A worldwide study of marine biodiversity, called the Census of Marine Life, was conducted between 2000 and 2010. Scientists from 82 countries worked to record the diversity, **distribution** and number of marine species, both in the past and today. Scientists explored ocean canyons, seamounts and under the polar ice. They tracked **migratory** animals, such as whales and tuna. From 2003 to 2009, Census of Marine Life scientists discovered 5722 new marine species living at depths of 1000 metres or more.

Census of Marine Life scientists have discovered thousands of new species, such as the white-topped coral crab. The Census of Marine Life is the first listing of species found in the world's oceans.

Did you know?

There are 16 000 known species of marine fish. Scientists believe there may be about 4000 species yet to be discovered, mainly in **tropical** seas.

Seamount biodiversity

Seamounts are areas of very high biodiversity. They are undersea mountains that rise 1000 metres or more from the deep ocean floor, but do not reach the surface of the water.

Many marine species depend on seamounts. Seamount biodiversity is high because seamounts:

- provide **habitats** at a wide range of depths, so different animal species that live at different depths are found there
- are formed from volcanic eruptions, so they are very rocky, unlike the ocean floor, which is mostly soft mud. Corals and sponges can find a firm place to attach to a seamount, and many other species can find shelter there too.
- affect ocean **currents**, forcing them to carry **nutrients** up from the ocean floor. These nutrients support a rich food web, from tiny plankton to fish, whales and seabirds.

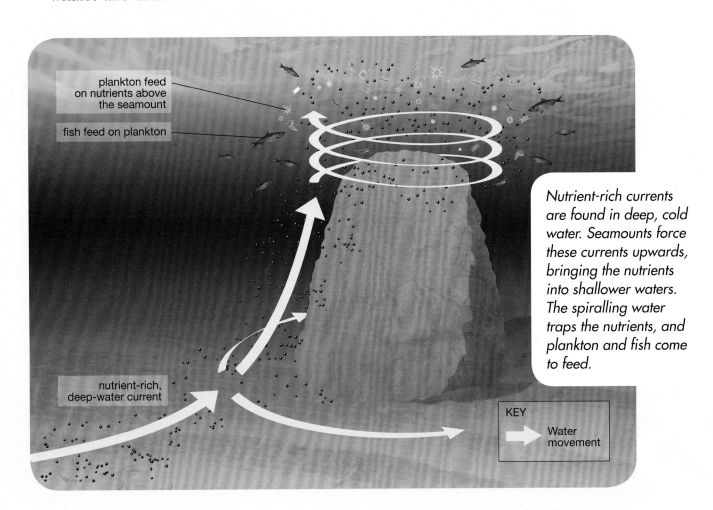

plankton feed on nutrients above the seamount

fish feed on plankton

nutrient-rich, deep-water current

Nutrient-rich currents are found in deep, cold water. Seamounts force these currents upwards, bringing the nutrients into shallower waters. The spiralling water traps the nutrients, and plankton and fish come to feed.

KEY

Water movement

Ocean and sea ecosystems

Living and non-living things, and the **interactions** between them, make up ocean and sea **ecosystems**. Living things are plants and animals. Non-living things are rocks, water, **currents** and the **climate**.

Food chains and food webs

A very important way that different **species** interact is by eating or consuming other species. This transfers energy and **nutrients** from one **organism** to another. A food chain illustrates this flow of energy, by showing what eats what. Food chains are best set out in a diagram. A food web shows how many different food chains fit together.

This Southern Ocean food web is made up of several food chains. In one food chain, plankton are eaten by whiting, which are eaten by bottlenose dolphins, which are eaten by orca.

Did you know?

In the Mediterranean Sea, fishing has reduced fish populations. This has meant that sea jelly numbers have increased, because there is more food for them now that they do not have to compete with as many fish for food.

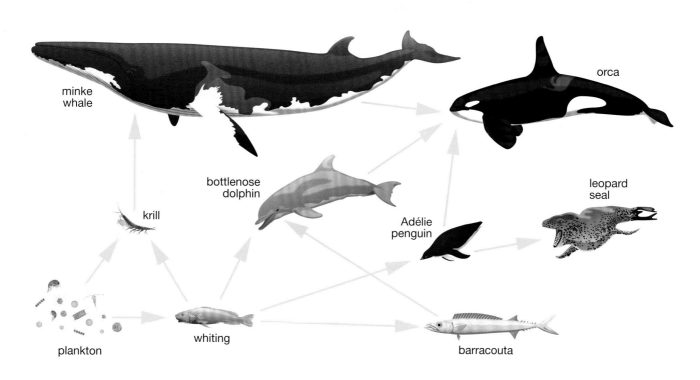

minke whale

orca

bottlenose dolphin

leopard seal

krill

Adélie penguin

plankton

whiting

barracouta

Remora fish interact with large sharks by hitching rides. A remora has a pad on its head that sticks to the shark. It gets free transport and feeds on scraps when the shark makes a kill. Here, two remora hitch a ride.

Other interactions

Living things in an ocean interact in other ways, too. Vast **shoals** of anchovies and herring are food for many ocean **predators**. Dolphins locate these shoals using echolocation, where they send out high-pitched sounds that bounce off the fish, helping them to locate the fish. They herd the fish into a tight ball, close to the ocean surface, to keep their prey from escaping. When this happens, seabirds such as gannets can reach the fish, too. Sharks and barracoutas also join in to feed on the shoal. With the prey gathered in a tight ball, a whale may take the opportunity to swallow the fish with a single gulp.

Human and dolphin interaction

In the Brazilian coastal city of Laguna, bottlenose dolphins drive fish to the shore, where fishers wait with nets. The humans make their catch and the dolphins feed on the fish that flee back out to sea. This cooperative fishing has been going on since 1847. Similar cooperation between bottlenose dolphins and humans occurs in Mauritania, in western Africa.

13

Threats to oceans and seas

Ocean and sea biodiversity is under threat from a range of human activities, such as overfishing, oil and chemical pollution and plastics pollution. **Climate** change is affecting oceans in ways that are complex and not yet fully understood.

Biodiversity hotspots

There are about 34 land areas in the world that have been identified as biodiversity hotspots. These are regions on land with a high number of **endemic species** and where biodiversity is under severe threat. **Marine** areas that have high biodiversity are coral reefs and **seamounts**. Seamounts also have high numbers of endemic species, because they are like underwater islands of biodiversity in the ocean. This is because species evolve on one particular seamount, and they are not able to spread out and reach other **habitats** because of the vastness of the ocean.

Locating seamounts

It is very important to locate seamounts so that these vital marine habitats can be protected. At least 14 000 seamounts are known to exist. The ocean floor has not yet been fully mapped, however, and some scientists predict that there may be up to 100 000 seamounts in the world's oceans and seas.

Coral reefs have the highest biodiversity of any ocean habitat, but many are under threat.

Threats to ocean and sea biodiversity

The major threat to seamount biodiversity is overfishing. Seamounts are habitats for many fish species that are caught for human consumption, such as yellowfin tuna. The overfishing of a species around a seamount can change the **ecosystem** of the seamount.

Other threats to ocean and sea biodiversity are plastics pollution, oil spills and chemical pollution, ocean acidification and ocean warming. Oceans need to be protected because they:

- are habitats for many species
- contain 90 per cent of the total number of living things on Earth
- are the major source of **protein** for one billion people
- produce half of the world's oxygen.

The endangered Florida manatee is threatened by collisions with boats, oil spills and siltation of the sea floor where it feeds. Siltation is when soil and sediments build up in an area.

BIODIVERSITY THREAT:
Overfishing

Every year, around 4 million fishing boats take a total of at least 85 million tonnes of animals from the world's oceans. Most are for eating. Popular **species** are fished to the point of **extinction**, and other species are at risk because they are caught accidentally.

Harvested fish species

Many fish species are **harvested**, or fished for human use. Scientists estimate that about 50 per cent of these species are overfished, which means that their populations are declining and they are at risk of extinction.

Southern bluefin tuna

Southern bluefin tuna is very popular for eating. In 1961, 1.2 million southern bluefin tuna were caught. By 1993, catch numbers had fallen, because the species had become harder to find. In 1994, countries that fished this tuna, such as Japan, Australia and New Zealand, agreed to set strict **quotas** on how many they would catch. In 2009, scientists estimated that the species was at risk of becoming extinct.

Harvested marine animals

TYPE OF **MARINE** ANIMAL	EXAMPLES	APPROXIMATE NUMBER OF TONNES CAUGHT EACH YEAR

Fish:
   Open-water fish
   Bottom-living fish
	Herring, tuna, anchovies, sardines, sharks
	 Orange roughy, haddock, flounder, cod
		More than 75 million

Crustaceans	Prawns, crab, lobsters, krill	4 million
Molluscs	Squid, octopus	3 million
Mammals	Whales, dolphins, porpoises, seals	Less than one million

Bycatch

Animals that are accidentally caught by fishers are called bycatch. Most types of commercial fishing produce bycatch.

In longline fishing, baited hooks are trailed behind a boat. Seabirds lunge for the bait before it sinks, and many are hooked and dragged under. As many as 300 000 seabirds drown in this way each year.

In trawl fishing, a net is dragged across the sea floor to catch species such as prawns. Sponges, rays and other species are also caught. They are thrown back overboard, often dead.

Gillnets are large nets that hang upright in the ocean. Any fish or mammal that tries to swim through the net may be trapped and drown. In 2010, gillnetting was banned in the southern Pacific Ocean. Gillnets that are longer than 2.5 kilometres are called drift nets. They have been banned worldwide since 1991.

Tuna bycatch

Tuna fishing once caused the deaths of up to 80 000 dolphins a year. From 1986, after a publicity campaign, tuna companies agreed to change their fishing practices. Since then, many cans of tuna have been labelled 'dolphin-safe', meaning that no dolphins were killed when the tuna was caught.

BIODIVERSITY THREAT:
Plastics pollution

Plastics and materials such as polystyrene pose a major threat to **marine** biodiversity. These materials take a long time to break down. Before they do so, they can entangle, choke or poison marine animals.

Synthetic materials

Plastics and polystyrene are types of synthetic materials. Synthetic materials are non-natural, human-produced materials, which do not break down quickly like natural materials do.

Nurdles

Nurdles are small plastic pellets that are about 5 millimetres or less across. They are used to make plastic items. About 100 million tonnes of nurdles are produced each year and shipped around the world to factories. Many find their way into the oceans when ships have accidents or spillages. On some beaches, nurdles are the most common beach **pollutant**, as well as plastic particles that have worn off larger pieces of plastic waste.

Nurdles can choke or poison marine life. The nurdles absorb deadly factory and farming pollutants from sea water. When animals swallow nurdles, they are poisoned by the pollutants in them.

How plastic and other synthetic materials kill marine animals

THREAT	PLASTIC OR SYNTHETIC ITEMS	EXAMPLES
Entanglement in the item	Shopping bags, fishing nets, packaging straps, six-pack holders	Animals may be unable to swim or fly if they become entangled, so they might not be able to catch prey or they may drown. Plastic can cut into flesh, leading to infection.
Choking or poisoning, after swallowing the item	Shopping bags, cigarette butts, nurdles, polystyrene packaging, cigarette butts	Animals swallow items, which may block their intestines, choke them or poison them. Leatherback turtles mistake plastic bags for their jellyfish prey. Whales may accidentally swallow items when feeding. Birds may mistake cigarette butts for food and swallow them. Nurdles may be swallowed by birds, fish and krill.

Great Pacific Garbage Patch

Ocean **currents** concentrate plastics and litter into areas called **gyres**. There are five major gyres in the world. The gyre in the northern Pacific Ocean is up to one-fifth the size of the United States. It has so much plastic in it that the area is called the Great Pacific Garbage Patch. Most of this plastic is in pieces that are barely visible to the naked eye. These nurdles and the poisons they carry enter the ocean food web, which includes many humans who feed on fish caught in this region.

In 2009, an expedition took 100 seawater samples over a voyage of 3000 kilometres through the Great Pacific Garbage Patch. They found synthetic materials in every sample. Large items included plastic bottles, shoe soles, buckets, chairs, polystyrene pieces and great tangles of fishing net.

Did you know?

About 80 per cent of plastic and synthetic material in the oceans is washed into the water from the land. The rest is accidentally washed overboard or dumped deliberately from boats.

The Great Pacific Garbage Patch is created by a large gyre. The gyre's currents draw in litter from the ocean around it, and the currents gradually move the litter toward the centre of the gyre, where it is trapped.

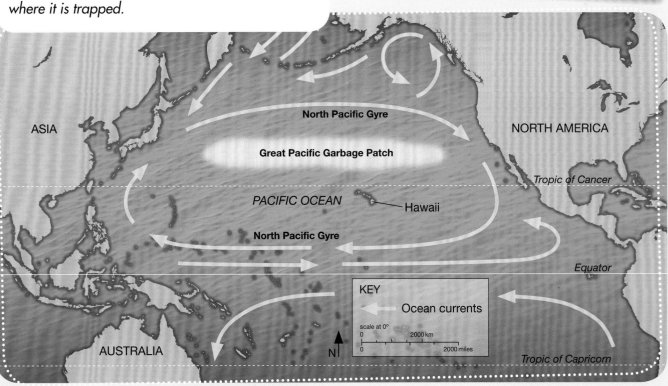

BIODIVERSITY THREAT:
Oil and chemical pollution

Major oil spills, from large tankers, kill huge numbers of **marine** animals. However, most oil pollution, like chemical pollution, is washed into the oceans from the land.

Oil pollution

Oil does not dissolve in water and so it floats as a slick on the water surface. Tanker and oil rig accidents contribute only about 15 per cent of the total amount of oil that enters the oceans every year. Another 30 per cent comes from minor leaks from ships. The main source is run-off from city streets.

How oil affects marine life

Oil may affect a marine animal by clogging its feathers or fur. An animal's fur helps it hold in its body heat, and fur clogged with oil cannot do this. Birds with oil-soaked feathers cannot fly.

Oil that is swallowed can damage an animal's internal organs, and oil fumes that are breathed in can damage lungs and nerves. Any oil that washes ashore may poison or harm land-breeding marine animals, such as birds and seals. Oil contains poisons that lead to disease and abnormal developments in animals. These chemicals remain in the marine environment for many years.

A sea otter lies back and feeds in oil-polluted water. The oil will clog the otter's fur and it may poison the otter too.

Chemical pollution

The worst chemical pollution comes from factory and farming waste that is discharged into rivers and drains that empty into oceans and seas. This chemical waste contains toxins, which are poisons. Many toxins take a very long time to break down into harmless substances.

Dead zones

Dead zones are areas of ocean and sea that are so low in oxygen that marine life dies. When farm fertilisers are washed into the sea, **phytoplankton** grow in large numbers very quickly and consume oxygen from the sea water. When the phytoplankton die, bacteria consume even more oxygen as they decompose them. This leaves very little oxygen in the water.

Organisms at the bottom of a food chain take in low levels of pollutants. Organisms higher on the chain have higher levels because they eats lots of the organisms that contain low levels. The higher an organism on the food chain, the more pollutants it accumulates, or builds up.

Bioaccumulation

Toxins are taken in by **organisms** and become concentrated in the body fat of animals at the top of the food chain. This is called bioaccumulation. Bioaccumulation is a major health threat to sharks, seals, whales and humans, because they are near the top of food chains and can accumulate toxins well above healthy levels. For this reason, some governments advise pregnant women and children to limit the amount of tuna and other **predatory** fish that they eat.

Did you know?

There may be 400 dead zones in the world. The largest is in the Gulf of Mexico and covers an area of 22 000 square kilometres.

Bioaccumulation of pollutants

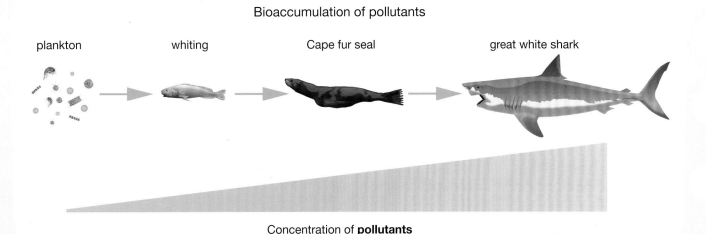

plankton   whiting   Cape fur seal   great white shark

Concentration of **pollutants**

BIODIVERSITY THREAT:
Carbon dioxide

The world's average temperature is rising because levels of certain gases, such as **carbon dioxide**, are increasing in Earth's atmosphere. These gases trap heat and cause **climate** change. Increasing levels of carbon dioxide are also making oceans more acidic.

Increasing levels of carbon dioxide

Carbon dioxide is found naturally in the atmosphere. Over the past 200 years, the level of this gas has increased noticeably. This is because humans have been burning fossil fuels such as oil and coal. These fuels are mostly made up of carbon, which is converted to carbon dioxide when it is burned. The increasing atmospheric levels of carbon dioxide and certain other gases are causing an increase in the average temperature of the world's oceans. It is also causing the oceans to become more acidic.

Ocean acidification

When carbon dioxide is dissolved in water, it creates a weak acid, called carbonic acid. Oceans are becoming more acidic as sea water absorbs more carbon dioxide from the atmosphere.

As the oceans become more acidic, levels of calcium carbonate in the water fall. Calcium carbonate is the substance that marine animals such as oysters, prawns, and coral polyps use to make their shells. Less calcium carbonate means slower growth and weaker shells. This could cause some species to become extinct.

Did you know?

Oceans and seas have absorbed about half of all the carbon dioxide that has been released by the burning of fossil fuels since 1800.

Coral reefs may die when increased carbon dioxide causes oceans and seas to become warmer or more acidic. Many coral reef species will lose their **habitats**.

Ocean warming

As ocean temperatures rise, ocean **currents** will change and marine species will be affected in many ways. **Phytoplankton** produce half the world's oxygen. They are the foundation of ocean food chains, and they are eaten by other plankton, crabs, shellfish, and small fish, which in turn are eaten by larger **predators**. Phytoplankton are also eaten by krill, which is the major food of baleen whales. Changes in ocean temperature and currents will affect the number and **distribution** of phytoplankton. In turn, this will affect the number and distribution of many other ocean species.

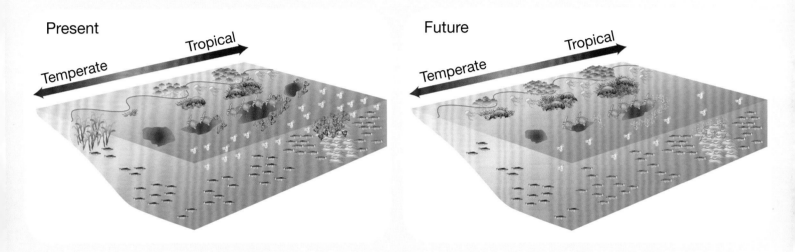

These diagrams show how ocean biodiversity looks now and how it may change in the future. Ocean warming will affect both **temperate** *and* **tropical** *seas.*

Marine turtles

All seven species of marine turtles are endangered. Climate change may affect their breeding. As temperatures rise, the polar icecaps are melting and sea levels are rising. Turtle nesting beaches may be washed away. The sex of turtle nestlings is determined by temperature. A rise in temperature by just 1 or 2 degrees Celsius will increase the number of hatchlings that are female. This could affect breeding.

Ocean and sea conservation

Conservation is the protection, preservation and wise use of resources. Conserving ocean and sea biodiversity involves protecting it from threats caused by human activities. Research, education and laws are very important to ocean conservation.

Research

Research surveys or studies are used to find out information about oceans and seas, such as how ocean **ecosystems** work and how humans affect them. This research helps people work out ways to conserve oceans. Most of the floor of the oceans has not been explored yet, but new technology is making it possible for research scientists to explore depths that could not be reached before.

Education

Educating people about oceans is essential for ocean conservation. Information from scientists must be passed on to people, such as students, fishers and tourists. If people are shown how oceans are important, they will be more likely to help conserve them.

Researching the past

Scientists may study museum specimens and historical records, such as newspaper cuttings. These things can give scientists clues about the number and **distribution** of **species** in the past. From past records, scientists can estimate that before whaling began in the 1800s around 27 000 southern right whales lived in the Tasman Sea, east of Australia. Today, about 1000 of these animals are found there.

Research scientists test the water in the Arctic Ocean. They may be testing for ocean acidity.

24

It is very difficult and expensive to find, catch and stop illegal fishing boats because the ocean is so large.

Laws

There are many laws to protect **marine** areas, but illegal fishing remains a major problem. Prices for rare and popular fish are often high, and some fishers are prepared to ignore laws and fishing limits to make money. They may catch undersized fish, use illegal nets that may harm other species or dump waste overboard.

Marine Protected Areas

Marine Protected Areas (MPAs) are areas of ocean that have been set aside for conservation and protected by law. Different MPAs have different levels of protection. Some are 'no-take' areas where all fishing is banned. In others, fishing may be allowed but shipping might be restricted. In 2009, there were about 5000 MPAs but, in total, these covered less than 1 per cent of the world's oceans.

Cleaning up the oceans

One part of conservation is cleaning up the damage that has already been done. In March 2009, Project Kaisei was launched. Its aim is to study marine garbage to work out how it might be cleaned up. The project focuses on the Great Pacific Garbage Patch.

CASE STUDY:
The Red Sea

The Red Sea is a **tropical** sea. It has many different **habitats**, such as shallow waters where coral reefs and seagrass meadows grow, and areas that are more than 2000 metres deep and support more than 42 deep-sea fish **species**.

Red Sea biodiversity

The Red Sea has the greatest proportion of **endemic species** of any sea in the world. This is due to several factors, such as:

- it is one of the warmest and saltiest of the world's seas, and particular Red Sea species have **adapted** to these conditions
- it is partly separated from the open ocean, which helps to keep Red Sea species and other ocean species apart.

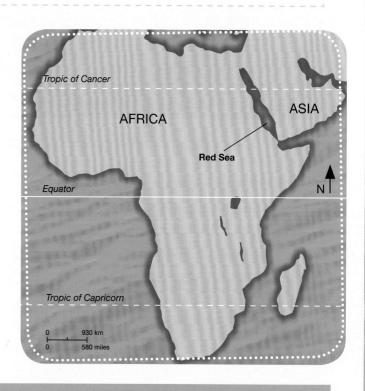

The Red Sea lies between Africa and Asia. It has 2000 kilometres of coral reef along its coasts, providing habitats for many species.

Animal species in the Red Sea

TYPE OF ANIMAL	NUMBER OF SPECIES	COMMENT
Fish	1350, including 44 shark species	17% are endemic species
Corals	More than 260	20% are endemic species
Cetaceans (such as whales and dolphins)	At least 16	None are endemic species
Turtles	5	It is home to five of the world's seven **marine** turtle species
Dugong	1	The dugong depends on seagrass meadows

Threats to Red Sea biodiversity

Threats to Red Sea biodiversity come from the human population. Offshore oil fields and resorts and towns along the coast pollute the sea. Illegal fishing is reducing numbers of some species.

Oil drilling and coastal development

There are at least 26 oil fields in the Red Sea. Marine life around them has been severely reduced by oil leakage.

The largest city on the coast is Jeddah, in Saudi Arabia, with a population of 3.5 million. Around 800 million litres of waste water, including **sewage**, is discharged into the sea every day from Jeddah. Desalination plants, which create fresh water from sea water, release more than 2 billion litres of hot, very salty water every day. Coral reefs are damaged by this pollution.

Illegal fishing

Over the past 20 years, shark numbers have fallen due to illegal fishing. Many sharks are caught and then have their dorsal fins cut off to be sold for shark-fin soup. The rest of the still-living animal is dumped overboard. Egypt and other Red Sea countries have banned shark fishing, but high prices for shark fins remain and fishers are prepared to risk being caught. Other fish that are taken illegally from the Red Sea are coral reef species, which are sold as aquarium pets around the world.

Did you know?

Every year, up to 100 million sharks are killed in the world's oceans and seas.

Oil spills and other pollution in the Red Sea can poison the seagrass that dugongs feed on.

Pollution

The Red Sea's narrow opening prevents ocean **currents** from circulating its water, so pollution that enters the Red Sea is not quickly flushed out. The sea is also quite small, so levels of **pollutants** can rise quickly.

The Black Sea, between Turkey and Europe, is similar in size to the Red Sea and it is also cut off from ocean currents. In the past 100 years, pollution and **invasive species** have caused a high loss of Black Sea biodiversity and a decline in important commercial fish species. A similar situation could occur in the Red Sea if its biodiversity is not protected.

The Suez Canal and invasive species

The Suez Canal is a shipping canal that opened in 1869, joining the Mediterranean and Red seas. The Red Sea is 1.2 metres higher than the Mediterranean, so water flows in that direction, carrying Red Sea species with it. Many of these have spread through the eastern Mediterranean, taking over from native species. Very few species have moved the other way, from the Mediterranean Sea to the Red Sea.

Pollution that enters the Red Sea becomes trapped and collects along the shore.

Coastal development around the Red Sea is a major threat, but countries are developing conservation plans to protect biodiversity.

Conserving Red Sea biodiversity

Countries that have Red Sea shoreline cooperate to protect **marine** biodiversity. They are members of PERSGA, which is the Regional Organization for the Conservation of the Environment of the Red Sea and Gulf of Aden. The main threats to biodiversity that PERSGA addresses are:

- coastal development
- waste disposal
- illegal fishing, especially of sharks
- overfishing
- managing oil tankers to avoid spills.

Through PERSGA, countries have established Marine Protected Areas (MPAs) and developed conservation plans for important species such as marine turtles. PERSGA is also involved in studies of sharks, fisheries and coral reefs. Red Sea countries can use these studies to help them make conservation decisions. PERSGA provides education programs for schools and training programs for industries that affect the Red Sea and its biodiversity.

What is the future for oceans and seas?

Oceans and seas are under severe threat from human activities. The problems of overfishing, increasing **carbon dioxide** and pollution are great, but you can contribute to ocean and sea conservation.

What can you do for oceans and seas?

You can help protect oceans and seas in many ways.

- Be a responsible consumer, and buy items that have little or no packaging.
- Dispose of litter properly. Much of the plastic rubbish in the Great Pacific Garbage Patch is litter that was discarded in city streets.
- Participate in coastal clean-up days or join a **marine** conservation organisation.
- If you eat fish, buy only fish **species** that are not threatened.
- If you are concerned about ocean conservation issues, write to or email your local newspaper, your local member of parliament or another politician. Know what you want to say, set out your arguments, be sure of your facts and ask for a reply.

Useful websites

🖥 **http://www.coml.org**
The Census of Marine Life website has information on the latest marine discoveries and past and current projects.

🖥 **http://www.biodiversityhotspots.org**
This website has information about the richest and most threatened areas of biodiversity on Earth.

🖥 **http://www.iucnredlist.org**
The IUCN Red List has information about threatened plant and animal species.

Glossary

adapt   change in order to survive

carbon dioxide   a colourless and odourless gas produced by plants and animals

climate   the weather conditions in a certain region over a long period of time

current   body of water moving in a certain direction

distribution   area where an animal or plant is found

ecosystem   the living and non-living things in a certain area and the interactions between them

endemic species   species found only in a particular area

extinct   having no living members

gene   segment of deoxyribonucleic acid (DNA) in the cells of a living thing, which determines its characteristics

gyre   circular pattern of currents in an ocean

habitat   place where animals, plants or other living things live

harvest   gather for human use, such as eating

heritage   things we inherit and pass on to following generations

interaction   action that is taken together or actions that affect each other

invasive species   non-native species that spread through habitats

landlocked   enclosed by land

marine   of the sea

migrate   move from one place to another, especially seasonally

nutrient   chemical that is used by living things for growth

organism   animal, plant or other living thing

phytoplankton   microscopic plants that drift in the sea

pollutant   harmful or poisonous human-produced substance that enters an environment, possibly causing damage to organisms

predator   animal that kills and eats other animals

protein   chemicals that are an essential part of all living things

quota   limit

seamounts   undersea mountains on the ocean floor that do not reach the water's surface

sewage   human and animal waste

shoal   group of fish swimming together

species   a group of animals, plants or other living things that share the same characteristics and can breed with one another

temperate   in a region or climate that has mild temperatures

tropical   in the hot and humid region between the Tropic of Cancer and the Tropic of Capricorn

Index